DOUGHNUTS

Delicious recipes for finger-licking treats

DOUGHNUTS

Delicious recipes for finger-licking treats

HANNAH MILES

Photography by
WILLIAM LINGWOOD

LONDON • NEW YORK

For Hunter Miles, a very special little girl x

DESIGNER Clare Barber
EDITOR Rebecca Woods
PRODUCTION Patricia Harrington
ART DIRECTOR Leslie Harrington
EDITORIAL DIRECTOR Julia Charles

PROP STYLIST Liz Belton
FOOD STYLIST Lucy Mckelvie
INDEXER Hilary Bird

First published in 2012
by Ryland Peters & Small
20–21 Jockey's Fields
London WC1R 4BW
and
519 Broadway, 5th Floor
New York, NY 10012
www.rylandpeters.com

Text © Hannah Miles 2012
Design and photographs
© Ryland Peters & Small 2012
Printed in China

10 9 8 7 6 5 4 3 2 1

ISBN: 978-1-84975-251-0

A CIP record for this book is available from the British Library.

US Library of Congress Cataloging-in-publication data has
been applied for.

AUTHOR'S ACKNOWLEDGMENTS:
With many thanks to Ryland Peters & Small, particularly Julia Charles
for allowing me to indulge my doughnut dreams, Rebecca Woods for the
patient editing and Leslie Harrington and Clare Barber for the beautiful
book design and art direction. With thanks to William Lingwood for the
stunning photography and to Lucy Mckelvie for baking such delicious-
looking doughnuts. Thanks also to Liz Belton for the pretty prop styling
and to Lauren and JJ for all their hard work publicizing this book. Love
and hugs to Heather, Elly and Claire from HHB Agency who are with
me every step of the way. Particular thanks to Merrin Ashcroft for all the
wonderful doughnut tips and advice—you were my knight in shining
armour and this book would not have been written without you! And to
my doughnut tasters—the Lidlington Allotment association, Podington
Sewing Circle and all my friends and family—a HUGE thank you for
going beyond the call of duty and eating so many doughnuts!

NOTES
• All spoon measurements are level, unless otherwise specified.
• Eggs are medium unless otherwise specified. Uncooked or partially
cooked eggs should not be served to the very old, frail, young children,
pregnant women or those with compromised immune systems.
• When a recipe calls for the grated zest of citrus fruit, buy unwaxed fruit
and wash well before using. If you can only find treated fruit, scrub well
in warm soapy water before using.
• If doughnuts are filled with fresh cream, ensure they are stored in a
refrigerator until ready to serve.

CONTENTS

Lip-smacking Delights

Doughnuts, whether fried, baked or batter, are a naughty, but very nice, indulgence! Popular the world over—from the Krispy Kremes made famous by New York TV series *Sex and the City*, to the battered delights served warm in Asian street markets—whatever type of doughnut is your favorite, there is a delicious recipe in this book for you. Simple and easy to prepare at home, using standard kitchen equipment or newly available doughnut pans, these doughnuts are perfect for snacks, parties or even desserts.

There are several methods for preparing doughnuts. The most common doughnuts are made from a light yeast dough and fried, which although take time to prepare, are most definitely worth the wait. For a healthier option, oven baked doughnuts offer a lower fat content as they are not fried in oil. There are a variety of shaped pans available in good kitchen stores for baked doughnuts, which give them a classic doughnut ring shape. You can also make doughnuts with a batter similar to that used for waffles or thick pancakes. These can either be made using a batter dispenser to drop rings of batter into hot oil or using a doughnut machine. Doughnut machines are relatively inexpensive and work similarly to a waffle iron. They produce doughnuts very quickly and are therefore ideal for large scale doughnut production—such as for the Doughnut Croquembouche on page 43.

I have to confess that, at first attempt, making traditional fried doughnuts can seem a little daunting and there are a few things that can go wrong. However, the steps in this book simplify the process and will ensure that you make perfect doughnuts every time. One of the key steps is the right combination of flour for your doughnut base—whilst you can use strong/bread flour on its own, the best results use a combination of this and ordinary all-purpose/plain flour to give lightness to the dough.

An essential step in making perfect fried doughnuts is the kneading process. Do not underestimate the time you must knead the dough for. To save time (and your arms), this is best done with a stand mixer fitted with a dough hook. Using the dough hook, you need to work the dough slowly for about 2 minutes and then increase the speed and knead vigorously for about another 8 minutes. When done, the dough will be very soft but not sticky and when you pull a piece between your hands it should be thin and elastic and not break or create holes. The next stage is resting and proving. Shape the dough into balls (or rings, depending on which doughnut you are making) and place each one on a flour-dusted square of baking parchment. Cover with a clean damp kitchen towel and leave to rest for 10 minutes, allowing the dough to relax, then reshape so that you have perfectly round doughnuts. Next, cover the trays in lightly-oiled plastic wrap/clingfilm and let rise in a warm place until doubled in size. The actual proving time required will be influenced by how warm it is. In my kitchen, which is warm from the Aga, the proving takes about 35 minutes. To test if the dough is proved, press one of the doughnuts gently with a fingertip. If the dent springs back, the dough is not yet fully proved. If the dent just holds it shape, the doughnuts are ready. If you press and the dough collapses, the doughnuts are over proved and will taste yeasty and may deflate slightly when you put them into the oil. The final stage is to let the doughnuts rest uncovered for another 10 minutes before frying to allow a thin crust to form.

When frying doughnuts you need the oil to be very hot 375°F (190°C). This is easiest done in a deep fat fryer, where the temperature can be controlled, but you can also fry them, carefully, in a large saucepan on the hob using a kitchen thermometer to ensure the oil is at the right temperature. When it comes to adding the doughnuts to the pan, this is where the baking parchment helps. If the dough is handled too much it can deflate, so lifting the doughnuts by gripping the individual squares of parchment lets you slide them, one at a time, safely into the oil without deflating the dough or burning yourself. Cook the doughnuts for a couple of minutes on one side until golden brown, then turn over and cook until golden on the other side. Doing this will create the classic pale ring around the middle of the doughnut.

When filling doughnuts, it is important to make a cavity in the doughnut which is large enough to hold plenty of filling—there is nothing worse than a meanly-filled doughnut! This is best done with a round-handled teaspoon—poke it into the side of the doughnut and then move around to create a cavity inside, whilst keeping the exterior hole as small as you can. The easiest way to fill doughnuts is to use a piping bag, otherwise things can get a bit messy! Pipe the filling into the doughnut until you feel the doughnut slightly "kick back" in your hand, which means that it is full. Don't worry too much if you over-fill as you can simply wipe away any excess with a paper towel. If you are filling your doughnuts with fresh cream, always remember to store them in the fridge until ready to serve.

Baked and batter doughnuts are simpler to make as they do not contain yeast and therefore don't require proving time—perfect for those sudden doughnut cravings!

All doughnuts taste better fresh and are best served the day they are made. But if you don't manage this (despite how irresistible they are!) store them in an airtight container. Whichever type of doughnut you prefer, these recipes will enable you to create decadent delights at home to treat friends and family—the only issue is how to stop eating them—you have been warned!

FUN-FILLED TREATS

Traditional Jelly Doughnuts

A jelly doughnut to me is the classic—dusted in sugar and oozing with strawberry or raspberry jelly when you bite into the middle. It is always best to serve these doughnuts fresh and make sure that you fill them generously—there is nothing worse than a meanly-filled doughnut! By turning them over halfway through cooking, you should end up with the classic white line around the perimeter of the doughnut, making them look just as good as store-bought doughnuts.

¾ cup/200 ml milk, warm
¼ oz./7 g fast-action dried yeast
2½ tablespoons/30 g granulated sugar
2⅓ cups/300 g all-purpose/plain flour, plus extra for dusting
1¼ cups/160 g white bread/strong flour
½ teaspoon salt
2 eggs, beaten
4 tablespoons/60 g butter, softened
sunflower oil, for greasing and frying
superfine/caster sugar, for dusting
16 oz./450 g strawberry or raspberry jelly/jam

16 small squares of baking parchment
a piping bag with a round tip/nozzle

MAKES 16

Whisk together the warm milk, yeast and sugar in a pitcher/jug and leave in a warm place for about 10 minutes until a thick foam has formed on top of the milk. Meanwhile, sift the flours into a large mixing bowl, add the salt, eggs and butter and stir together, then pour in the yeast mixture. Using a stand mixer fitted with a dough hook, mix the dough on a slow speed for 2 minutes, then increase the speed and knead for about 8 minutes until the dough is soft and pliable. Alternatively, knead the dough by hand for 15 minutes. The mixture will be very soft but should not be sticky, so dust with flour if needed.

Lay the squares of baking parchment on a tray and lightly dust with flour. Divide the dough into 16 portions and, dusting your hands with flour, shape each portion into a ball and place one on each square of parchment. Cover the doughnuts with a clean damp kitchen towel and leave to rest for 10 minutes. Reshape the balls and then let rise in a warm place for about 35–45 minutes, covered in lightly-greased plastic wrap, until the dough has doubled in size and holds an indent when you press with a fingertip. Rest again, uncovered, for 10 minutes.

In a large saucepan or deep fat fryer, heat the oil to 375°F (190°C). Holding the square of parchment, transfer each doughnut to the pan, one at a time, being careful not to handle the dough or splash hot oil. Cook in small batches for about 1½ minutes on each side until golden brown. Remove the doughnuts from the oil using a slotted spoon and drain on paper towels.

When the doughnuts are cool enough to handle, pour the dusting sugar into a shallow dish and roll each doughnut in the sugar to coat thoroughly. Use a round teaspoon handle to poke a hole in the doughnut and move it around to make a cavity inside. Spoon the jelly/jam into the piping bag and pipe into the cavity in each doughnut and serve.

Vanilla Cream Doughnuts

These classic doughnuts are simple but indulgent with delicate hints of vanilla and a rich creamy custard. Decorate with pretty sugar sprinkles for the perfect party treat.

¾ cup/200 ml milk, warm
¼ oz./7 g fast-action dried yeast
2½ tablespoons/30 g granulated sugar
2⅓ cups/300 g all-purpose/plain flour, plus extra for dusting
1¼ cups/160 g white bread/strong flour
½ teaspoon salt
2 eggs, beaten
4 tablespoons/60 g butter, softened
1 teaspoon vanilla extract
sunflower oil, for greasing and frying
sugar sprinkles, to decorate

FOR THE PASTRY CREAM

1 tablespoon cornstarch/cornflour
5 tablespoons/60 g sugar
1 egg plus 1 egg yolk
6½ tablespoons/100 ml milk
⅔ cup/150 ml heavy/double cream
1 vanilla bean/pod, split lengthwise

FOR THE FROSTING

5 tablespoons/70 ml vanilla syrup
1⅓ cups/200 g confectioners'/icing sugar, sifted

16 small squares of baking parchment
a piping bag with a round tip/nozzle

MAKES 16

Begin by preparing the pastry cream. In a mixing bowl, whisk together the cornstarch/cornflour, sugar, whole egg and egg yolk until creamy. Put the milk, cream and vanilla bean in a saucepan and bring to a boil. Turn off the heat and leave to infuse for 5 minutes then remove the vanilla bean and scrape out the seeds with a round-bladed knife. Return just the seeds to the pan and bring to a boil again. Slowly pour the hot milk and cream over the egg mixture, whisking all the time. Return the mixture to the pan and cook for a few minutes until thickened, then pass through a strainer/sieve to remove any lumps. Leave to cool then chill in the fridge until needed.

Whisk together the warm milk, yeast and sugar in a pitcher/jug and leave in a warm place for about 10 minutes until a thick foam has formed on top. Meanwhile, sift the flours into a mixing bowl, add the salt, eggs, butter and vanilla and stir together, then pour in the yeast mixture. Using a stand mixer fitted with a dough hook, mix on a slow speed for 2 minutes, then increase the speed and knead for 8 minutes until the dough is pliable. Alternatively, knead the dough by hand for 15 minutes. The mixture will be soft but should not be sticky, so dust with flour if needed.

Lay the squares of baking parchment on a tray and lightly dust with flour. Divide the dough into 16 portions and, dusting your hands with flour, shape each portion into a ball and place on a square of baking parchment. Cover the doughnuts with a clean damp kitchen towel and leave to rest for 10 minutes. Reshape the balls and then let rise in a warm place for about 35–45 minutes, covered in lightly-greased plastic wrap, until the dough has doubled in size and holds an indent when you press with a fingertip. Rest again, uncovered, for 10 minutes.

In a large saucepan or deep fat fryer, heat the oil to 375°F (190°C). Holding the square of parchment, transfer each doughnut to the pan, one at a time, being careful not to handle the dough or splash hot oil. Cook in small batches for about 1½ minutes on each side until golden brown, then remove from the oil with a slotted spoon and drain on paper towels.

When cool enough to handle, use a round teaspoon handle to poke a hole in the doughnut and move it around to make a cavity inside. Spoon the pastry cream into a piping bag and pipe into the doughnuts. For the frosting, whisk together the confectioners'/icing sugar and vanilla syrup until smooth and thick, adding a tablespoon of water to loosen, if necessary. Spread over the top of each doughnut, decorate with sugar sprinkles and serve.

Chocolate Indulgence Doughnuts

These doughnuts are a choc-a-holics delight: light chocolate dough with a glossy chocolate glaze topped with chocolate curls and filled with ever so naughty fresh whipped cream.

¾ cup/200 ml milk, warm

¼ oz./7 g fast-action dried yeast

2½ tablespoons/30 g granulated sugar

2 cups plus 2 tablespoons/280 g all-purpose/plain flour, plus extra for dusting

1¼ cups/160 g white bread/strong flour

⅓ cup/40 g unsweetened cocoa powder

½ teaspoon salt

2 eggs, beaten

4 tablespoons/60 g butter, softened

sunflower oil, for greasing and frying

1⅔ cups/400 ml heavy/double cream

chocolate curls, for decorating

FOR THE GLAZE

2. oz/60 g semi-sweet/plain chocolate

2 tablespoons/35 g butter

¼ cup/65 ml heavy/double cream

½ cup/70 g confectioners'/icing sugar, sifted

16 small squares of baking parchment

a piping bag with a round tip/nozzle

MAKES 16

Whisk together the warm milk, yeast and sugar in a pitcher/jug and leave in a warm place for about 10 minutes until a thick foam has formed on top of the milk. Meanwhile, sift the flours and cocoa powder into a large mixing bowl, add the salt, eggs and butter and stir together, then pour in the yeast mixture. Using a stand mixer fitted with a dough hook, mix the dough on a slow speed for 2 minutes, then increase the speed and knead for about 8 minutes until the dough is soft and pliable. Alternatively, knead the dough by hand for 15 minutes. The mixture will be very soft but should not be sticky, so dust with flour if needed.

Lay the squares of baking parchment on a tray and lightly dust with flour. Divide the dough into 16 portions and, dusting your hands with flour, shape each portion into a ball and place on a square of baking parchment. Cover the doughnuts with a clean damp kitchen towel and leave to rest for 10 minutes. Reshape the balls and then let rise in a warm place for about 35–45 minutes, covered in lightly-greased plastic wrap, until the dough has doubled in size and holds an indent when you press with a fingertip. Rest again, uncovered, for 10 minutes.

In a large saucepan or deep fat fryer, heat the oil to 375°F (190°C). Holding the square of parchment, transfer each doughnut to the pan, one at a time, being careful not to handle the dough or splash hot oil. Cook in small batches for about 1½ minutes on each side until golden brown. Remove the doughnuts from the oil using a slotted spoon and drain on paper towels.

When the doughnuts are cool, use a round teaspoon handle to poke a hole in the doughnut and move around to make a cavity inside. Whip the cream to stiff peaks then spoon it into the piping bag and pipe into the doughnuts. For the chocolate glaze, gently heat the chocolate, butter and cream in a saucepan, stirring, until you have a smooth, glossy sauce. Sift in the confectioners'/ icing sugar and beat well, ensuring there are no lumps. Dip the top of each doughnut into the glaze and sprinkle over the chocolate curls while still sticky, then leave in a cool place for the glaze to set. Serve or store in the fridge if not being eaten straight away.

Fall Pumpkin Doughnuts

¾ cup/200 ml milk, warm
¼ oz./7 g fast-action dried yeast
¼ cup/60 ml pure maple syrup
2⅓ cups/300 g all-purpose/plain flour, plus extra for dusting
1¼ cups/160 g white bread/strong flour
½ teaspoon salt
2 eggs, beaten
4 tablespoons/60 g butter, softened
1 teaspoon ground cinnamon
1 teaspoon ground ginger
a pinch of freshly grated nutmeg
sunflower oil, for greasing and frying
1¼ cups/300 ml heavy/double cream, whipped

FOR THE PUMPKIN CUSTARD
2 generous tablespoons cornstarch/cornflour
⅓ cup packed/60 g soft brown sugar
1 egg plus 1 egg yolk
1 cup/250 ml heavy/double cream
1 teaspoon ground cinnamon
1 teaspoon ground ginger
2 generous tablespoons pumpkin purée

FOR THE CANDIED PECANS
⅔ cup/120 g sugar
1 teaspoon vanilla extract
⅔ cup/100 g pecans, roughly chopped

16 small squares of baking parchment
2 piping bags with large star tips/nozzles

MAKES 16

These maple-scented doughnuts are filled with a warmly-spiced pumpkin custard and served with cream and candied pecans.

Begin by preparing the custard. In a mixing bowl, whisk together the cornstarch/cornflour, sugar, whole egg and egg yolk until creamy. Put the cream and spices in a saucepan and bring to the boil. Slowly pour this over the egg mixture, whisking all the time, then stir in the pumpkin purée. Return the mixture to the pan and cook for a few minutes until thickened, then pass through a sieve/strainer to remove any lumps. Leave to cool and chill in the fridge until needed.

For the candied pecans, heat the sugar and vanilla in a saucepan with ¼ cup/60 ml water, simmering until the sugar dissolves and you have a thin syrup. Add the pecans to the pan and cook until the sugar crystallizes. This will take about 20 minutes and will happen suddenly. Stir the nuts well and remove the pan from the heat. Set aside until needed.

Whisk together the warm milk, yeast and maple syrup in a pitcher/jug and leave in a warm place for about 10 minutes until a thick foam has formed on top. Meanwhile, sift the flours into a mixing bowl, add the salt, eggs, butter and spices and stir, then pour in the yeast mixture. Using a stand mixer fitted with a dough hook, mix the dough on a slow speed for 2 minutes, then increase the speed and knead for 8 minutes. Alternatively, knead the dough by hand for 15 minutes. The dough will be soft and pliable but should not be sticky, so dust with flour if needed.

Lay the squares of baking parchment on a tray and lightly dust with flour. Divide the dough into 16 portions and, dusting your hands with flour, roll each portion into an oblong shape and place on a square of baking parchment. Cover the doughnuts with a clean damp kitchen towel and leave to rest for 10 minutes. Reshape the oblongs and then let rise in a warm place for about 35–45 minutes, covered in lightly-greased plastic wrap, until the dough has doubled in size and holds an indent when you press with a fingertip. Rest again, uncovered, for 10 minutes.

In a large saucepan or deep fat fryer, heat the oil to 375°F (190°C). Holding the square of parchment, transfer each doughnut to the pan, one at a time, being careful not to handle the dough or splash hot oil. Cook in small batches for about 1½ minutes on each side until golden brown. Remove the doughnuts from the oil using a slotted spoon and drain on paper towels.

When you are ready to serve, use a knife to cut a lengthwise slit in the doughnut, being careful not to cut all the way through. Put the custard into one piping bag and the cream into the other and pipe a generous swirl of each into each doughnut then sprinkle with the candied pecans.

Cinnamon Cider Apple Doughnuts

These cinnamon spiced doughnuts are filled with apple purée and coated in a cider glaze. Served with a mug of warming mulled cider, they are the perfect fall treat.

¾ cup/200 ml milk, warm
¼ oz./7 g fast-action dried yeast
2½ tablespoons/30 g soft light brown sugar
2⅓ cups/300 g all-purpose/plain flour, plus extra for dusting
1¼ cups/160 g white bread/strong flour
½ teaspoon salt
2 eggs, beaten
4 tablespoons/60 g butter, softened
2 teaspoons ground cinnamon
sunflower oil, for greasing and frying

FOR THE FILLING
14 oz./400 g apple pie filling
1 tablespoon (hard) apple cider

FOR THE FROSTING AND APPLE DECORATION
1 small dessert apple, cored
scant ½ cup/100 ml sweet (hard) apple cider
2 cups/300 g confectioners'/icing sugar, sifted

16 small squares of baking parchment
a piping bag with a round tip/nozzle

MAKES 16

Whisk together the warm milk, yeast and sugar in a pitcher/jug and leave in a warm place for about 10 minutes until a thick foam has formed on top of the milk. Meanwhile, sift the flours into a large mixing bowl, add the salt, eggs, butter and cinnamon and stir together, then pour in the yeast mixture. Using a stand mixer fitted with a dough hook, mix the dough on a slow speed for 2 minutes, then increase the speed and knead for about 8 minutes until the dough is soft and pliable. Alternatively, knead the dough by hand for 15 minutes. The mixture will be very soft but should not be sticky, so dust with flour if needed.

Lay the squares of baking parchment on a tray and lightly dust with flour. Divide the dough into 16 portions and, dusting your hands with flour, shape each portion into a ball and place on a square of baking parchment. Cover them with a clean damp kitchen towel and leave to rest for 10 minutes. Reshape the balls and then let rise in a warm place for about 35–45 minutes, covered in lightly-greased plastic wrap, until the dough has doubled in size and holds an indent when you press with a fingertip. Rest again, uncovered, for 10 minutes.

In a large saucepan or deep fat fryer, heat the oil to 375°F (190°C). Holding the square of parchment, transfer each doughnut to the pan, one at a time, being careful not to handle the dough or splash hot oil. Cook in small batches for about 1½ minutes on each side until golden brown. Remove the doughnuts from the oil using a slotted spoon and drain on paper towels, then let cool on a wire rack.

When the doughnuts are cool, use a teaspoon handle to poke a hole in the doughnut and move around to make a cavity inside. Put the apple pie filling and cider in a food processor and blitz to a smooth purée, then spoon into the piping bag and pipe into the cavity of each doughnut.

Thinly slice the apple into rings using a mandolin or sharp knife. In a saucepan, heat the cider to a gentle simmer. Add the apple rings and simmer for a few minutes until the apples are just soft then remove them with a slotted spoon and drain on paper towels. Put the confectioners'/icing sugar in a bowl, add 3–4 tablespoons of the warm cider from the pan and stir until you have a smooth thick frosting. Spread the frosting over the top each doughnut using a round-bladed knife and decorate with an apple slice. Leave to set before serving.

Cherry Cheesecake Doughnuts

Cheesecakes are almost as popular as doughnuts so I have taken all the elements of a cheesecake—buttery crumb base, juicy fruit and creamy filling—and packed them into these indulgent little delights. These are a perfect dessert doughnut.

¾ cup/200 ml milk, warm
¼ oz./7 g fast-action dried yeast
2½ tablespoons/30 g granulated sugar
2⅓ cups/300 g all-purpose/plain flour, plus extra for dusting
1¼ cups/160 g white bread/strong flour
½ teaspoon salt
2 eggs, beaten
4 tablespoons/60 g butter, softened
sunflower oil, for greasing and frying

FOR THE FILLING
2 cups (16 oz.)/500 g mascarpone
1 cup/250 ml crème fraîche
3 tablespoons confectioners'/icing sugar, sifted
12 oz./270 g (drained weight) pitted morello cherries in light syrup

FOR THE CRUMB TOPPING
4 oz./125 g graham crackers/digestive biscuits
3 tablespoons/50 g butter

16 small squares of baking parchment
a piping bag with a round tip/nozzle
a piping bag with a star tip/nozzle

MAKES 16

Whisk together the warm milk, yeast and sugar in a pitcher/jug and leave in a warm place for about 10 minutes until a thick foam has formed on top of the milk. Meanwhile, sift the flours into a large mixing bowl, add the salt, eggs and butter and mix together to incorporate, then pour in the yeast mixture. Using a stand mixer fitted with a dough hook, mix the dough on a slow speed for 2 minutes, then increase the speed and knead for about 8 minutes until the dough is soft and pliable. Alternatively, knead the dough by hand for 15 minutes. The mixture will be very soft but should not be sticky, so dust with flour if needed.

Lay the squares of baking parchment on a tray and lightly dust with flour. Divide the dough into 16 portions and, dusting your hands with flour, shape each portion into a ball and place on a square of baking parchment. Cover the doughnuts with a clean damp kitchen towel and leave to rest for 10 minutes. Reshape the balls and then let rise in a warm place for about 35–45 minutes, covered in lightly-greased plastic wrap, until the dough has doubled in size and holds an indent when you press with a fingertip. Rest again, uncovered, for 10 minutes.

In a large saucepan or deep fat fryer, heat the oil to 375°F (190°C). Holding the square of parchment, transfer each doughnut to the pan, one at a time, being careful not to handle the dough or splash hot oil. Cook in small batches for about 1½ minutes on each side until golden brown. Remove the doughnuts from the oil using a slotted spoon and drain on paper towels. When the doughnuts are cool enough to handle, use a round teaspoon handle to poke a hole in the doughnut and move it around to make a cavity inside.

Whisk together the mascarpone, crème fraîche and confectioners'/icing sugar until smooth and creamy. Divide the mixture in half and set one half aside for the topping. Blitz half of the cherries to a smooth purée in a food processor and then fold into the remaining mascarpone mixture. Poke 3 or 4 of the reserved cherries into each doughnut, retaining 16 for decoration. Spoon the cherry mascarpone into the piping bag and pipe it into the cavity of each doughnut.

Spoon the plain mascarpone mixture into the piping bag fitted with a star nozzle and pipe stars onto the top of each doughnut. Blitz the crackers/biscuits to fine crumbs and stir in the melted butter. Sprinkle the buttery crumbs over the top of each doughnut and decorate with a cherry.

Pecan Pie Doughnuts

¾ cup/200 ml milk, warm
¼ oz./7 g fast-action dried yeast
¼ cup/60 ml maple syrup
2⅓ cups/300 g all-purpose/plain flour, plus extra for dusting
1¼ cups/160 g white bread/strong flour
½ teaspoon salt
2 eggs, beaten
4 tablespoons/60 g butter, softened
1 teaspoon vanilla extract
1 teaspoon ground cinnamon
sunflower oil, for greasing and frying

FOR THE CINNAMON CREAM
1 tablespoon cornstarch/cornflour
¼ cup plus 1 tablespoon/60 g sugar
1 egg plus 1 egg yolk
6½ tablespoons/100 ml milk
⅔ cup/150 ml heavy/double cream
1 teaspoon ground cinnamon

FOR THE PECAN PIE FILLING
2 tablespoons golden/light corn syrup
3 tablespoons/50 g butter
3 tablespoons/40 g soft brown sugar
3 tablespoons/40 g sugar
1 teaspoon ground cinnamon
1 teaspoon vanilla extract
1 egg, beaten
½ cup/60 g pecans, finely chopped

FOR THE PECAN SUGAR
¾ cup/150 g sugar
⅓ cup/50 g pecans, finely chopped
1 teaspoon ground cinnamon

16 small squares of baking parchment
2 piping bags with round tips/nozzles

MAKES 16

Sweet cinnamon custard and pecans enrobed in a buttery toffee sauce await when you bite into these decadent doughnuts.

Begin by preparing the cinnamon cream. Whisk together the cornstarch/flour, sugar, egg and egg yolk until creamy. Put the milk, cream and ground cinnamon in a saucepan and bring to a boil. Pour over the egg mixture, whisking all the time. Return to the pan and cook for a few minutes until thick. Pass through a sieve/strainer to remove any lumps and chill until needed.

For the pecan pie filling, heat the syrup, butter, sugars, cinnamon and vanilla in a saucepan until the butter has melted and the sugar is dissolved. Leave to cool for 10 minutes, then beat in the egg. Pass through a strainer/sieve, then stir in the pecans. Let cool then chill until needed.

Whisk together the warm milk, yeast and maple syrup in a pitcher/jug and leave in a warm place for 10 minutes until a thick foam has formed on top. Sift the flours into a mixing bowl, add the salt, eggs, butter, vanilla and cinnamon and stir, then pour in the yeast mixture. Using a stand mixer fitted with a dough hook, mix the dough on a slow speed for 2 minutes, then increase the speed and knead for 8 minutes. Alternatively, knead the dough by hand for 15 minutes. The dough will be soft and pliable but should not be sticky, so dust with flour if needed.

Lay the squares of baking parchment on a tray and lightly dust with flour. Divide the dough into 16 portions and, dusting your hands with flour, shape each portion into a ball and place on a square of baking parchment. Cover the doughnuts with a clean damp kitchen towel and leave to rest for 10 minutes. Reshape the balls and then let rise in a warm place for about 35–45 minutes, covered in lightly-greased plastic wrap, until the dough has doubled in size and holds an indent when you press with a fingertip. Rest again, uncovered, for 10 minutes.

In a large saucepan or deep fat fryer, heat the oil to 375°F (190°C). Holding the square of parchment, transfer each doughnut to the pan, one at a time, being careful not to handle the dough or splash hot oil. Cook in small batches for about 1½ minutes on each side until golden brown. Remove the doughnuts from the oil using a slotted spoon and drain on paper towels.

While the doughnuts are still warm, mix together the pecan sugar ingredients in a shallow dish and roll each doughnut in the mixture to coat. Use a round teaspoon handle to poke a hole in the doughnut and move it around to make a cavity inside. Stir the pecan pie filling, spoon into a piping bag and pipe a little of the mixture into each doughnut. Spoon the cinnamon custard into the other piping bag and pipe into each doughnut, filling the cavities, and serve.

Coffee Cream Doughnuts

A coffee cream doughnut is one of life's little treats—a caffeine hit and sugar rush all in one go! A perfect morning pick-me-up served with freshly brewed coffee.

¾ cup/200 ml milk, warm
¼ oz./7 g fast-action dried yeast
2½ tablespoons/30 g granulated sugar
2⅓ cups/300 g all-purpose/plain flour, plus extra for dusting
1¼ cups/160 g white bread/strong flour
½ teaspoon salt
2 eggs, beaten
4 tablespoons/60 g butter, softened
sunflower oil, for greasing and frying

FOR THE PASTRY CREAM

1 tablespoon cornstarch/cornflour
5 tablespoons/60 g sugar
1 egg plus 1 egg yolk
6½ tablespoons/100 ml milk
⅔ cup/150 ml heavy/double cream
1 tablespoon instant coffee granules

FOR THE FROSTING

2½ cups/350 g confectioners'/icing/sugar, sifted
2 tablespoons instant coffee granules dissolved in 3–4 tablespoons hot water
20 chocolate coffee beans

20 small squares of baking parchment
a piping bag with a round tip/nozzle

MAKES 20

Begin by preparing the pastry cream. In a mixing bowl, whisk together the cornstarch/cornflour, sugar, whole egg and egg yolk until creamy. Put the milk, cream and coffee granules in a saucepan set over gentle heat and warm, stirring, until the coffee has dissolved, then bring to a boil. Slowly pour this over the egg mixture, whisking all the time. Return the mixture to the pan and cook for a few minutes until thick, then pass through a strainer/sieve to remove any lumps. Let cool then chill until needed.

For the doughnuts, whisk together the warm milk, yeast and sugar in a jug/pitcher and leave in a warm place for about 10 minutes until a thick foam has formed on top. Meanwhile, sift the flours into a large mixing bowl, add the salt, eggs and butter and mix together to incorporate, then pour in the yeast mixture. Using a stand mixer fitted with a dough hook, mix the dough on a slow speed for 2 minutes, then increase the speed and knead for about 8 minutes until the dough is soft and pliable. Alternatively, knead the dough by hand for 15 minutes. The mixture will be very soft but should not be sticky, so dust with flour if needed.

Lay the squares of baking parchment on a tray and lightly dust with flour. Divide the dough into 20 portions and, dusting your hands with flour, shape each portion into a ball and place on a square of baking parchment. Cover the doughnuts with a clean damp kitchen towel and leave to rest for 10 minutes. Reshape the balls and then let rise in a warm place for about 35–45 minutes, covered in lightly-greased plastic wrap, until the dough has doubled in size and holds an indent when you press with a fingertip. Rest again, uncovered, for 10 minutes.

In a large saucepan or deep fat fryer, heat the oil to 375°F (190°C). Holding the square of parchment, transfer each doughnut to the pan, one at a time, being careful not to handle the dough or splash hot oil. Cook in small batches for about 1½ minutes on each side until golden brown. Remove the doughnuts from the oil using a slotted spoon and drain on paper towels.

When the doughnuts are cool, use a round teaspoon handle to poke a hole in the doughnut and move around to make a cavity inside. Spoon the pastry cream into a piping bag and pipe into the doughnuts. For the frosting, put the confectioners'/icing sugar in a bowl and add the coffee gradually (you may not need it all), stirring until you have a thick, spreadable frosting. Spread the frosting over the top of each doughnut and decorate with a chocolate coffee bean.

A HOLE LOT OF FUN!

Glazed Sugar Sprinkle Doughnuts

These delicious glazed vanilla doughnuts, decorated with cheerfully-colored sprinkles, are unbeatable for those who prefer to keep things simple.

¾ cup/200 ml milk, warm
¼ oz./7 g fast-action dried yeast
2½ tablespoons/30 g granulated sugar
2⅓ cups/300 g all-purpose/plain flour, plus extra for dusting
1¼ cups/160 g white bread/strong flour
½ teaspoon salt
2 eggs, beaten
4 tablespoons/60 g butter, softened
1 teaspoon vanilla extract
sunflower oil, for greasing and frying
sugar sprinkles, to decorate

FOR THE GLAZE
1½ cups/225 g confectioners'/icing sugar
pink food coloring (optional)

18 small squares of baking parchment
a ¾-inch/2-cm round cookie cutter

MAKES 18

Whisk together the warm milk, yeast and sugar in a pitcher/jug and leave in a warm place for about 10 minutes until a thick foam has formed on top of the milk. Meanwhile, sift the flours into a large mixing bowl, add the salt, eggs, butter and vanilla and stir together, then pour in the yeast mixture. Using a stand mixer fitted with a dough hook, mix the dough on a slow speed for 2 minutes, then increase the speed and knead for about 8 minutes until the dough is soft and pliable. Alternatively, knead the dough by hand for 15 minutes. The mixture will be very soft but should not be sticky, so dust with flour if needed.

Lay the squares of baking parchment on a tray and lightly dust with flour. Divide the dough into 16 portions and, dusting your hands with flour, roll into balls. Using the cookie cutter, cut out a hole from the centre of each dough ball to create a ring. Place each ring on a square of baking parchment. Combine the cut-out dough and mould into balls to make further rings—you should be able to make 18 in total. Cover the doughnuts with a clean damp kitchen towel and leave to rest for 10 minutes, and then let rise in a warm place for about 35–45 minutes, covered in lightly-greased plastic wrap, until the dough has doubled in size and holds an indent when you press with a fingertip. Rest again, uncovered, for 10 minutes.

In a large saucepan or deep fat fryer, heat the oil to 375°F (190°C). Holding the square of parchment, transfer each doughnut to the pan, one at a time, being careful not to handle the dough or splash hot oil. Cook in small batches for about 1½ minutes on each side until golden brown. Remove the doughnuts from the oil using a slotted spoon and drain on paper towels, then leave them to cool on a wire rack. Slide a sheet of foil under the rack to catch any drips of glaze later on.

Mix together the confectioners'/icing sugar, ⅓ cup/80 ml water and the food coloring, if using, to form a smooth thin glaze. Dip the top of each doughnut into the glaze to coat and scatter over the sugar sprinkles while the glaze is still sticky (it is best to do this in small batches as the glaze can set quickly). Leave to set before serving.

Lemon Ring Doughnuts

These zingy doughnuts, bursting with lemon, are a tasty treat. Drizzled with a tangy lemon glaze and decorated with sugar sprinkles, they look almost too pretty to eat. If you want to try making orange doughnuts, simply substitute orange zest and juice in place of the lemon.

¾ cup/200 ml milk, warm
¼ oz./7 g fast-action dried yeast
2½ tablespoons/30 g granulated sugar
2⅓ cups/300 g all-purpose/plain flour, plus extra for dusting
1¼ cups/160 g white bread/strong flour
½ teaspoon salt
2 eggs, beaten
4 tablespoons/60 g butter, softened
grated zest of 2 lemons
sunflower oil, for greasing and frying
sugar sprinkles, to decorate

FOR THE DIPPING GLAZE
freshly squeezed juice of 3 lemons
1 cup/150 g confectioners'/icing sugar, sifted

FOR THE FROSTING
⅔ cup/85 g confectioners'/icing sugar, sifted
freshly squeezed juice of 1 lemon
yellow food coloring

18 small squares of baking parchment
a ¾-inch/2-cm round cookie cutter
a piping bag with a small round tip/nozzle

MAKES 18

Whisk together the warm milk, yeast and sugar in a pitcher/jug and leave in a warm place for about 10 minutes until a thick foam has formed on top of the milk. Meanwhile, sift the flours into a large mixing bowl, add the salt, eggs, butter and lemon zest and stir together, then pour in the yeast mixture. Using a stand mixer fitted with a dough hook, mix the dough on a slow speed for 2 minutes, then increase the speed and knead for about 8 minutes until the dough is soft and pliable. Alternatively, knead the dough by hand. The mixture will be very soft but should not be sticky, so dust with flour if needed.

Lay the squares of baking parchment on a tray and lightly dust with flour. Divide the dough into 16 portions and, dusting your hands with flour, roll into balls. Using the cookie cutter, cut out a hole from the centre of each dough ball to create a ring. Place each ring on a square of baking parchment. Combine the cut-out dough and mould into balls to make further rings—you should be able to make 18 in total. Cover the rings with a clean damp kitchen towel and leave to rest for 10 minutes, and then let rise in a warm place for about 35–45 minutes, covered in lightly-greased plastic wrap, until the dough has doubled in size and holds an indent when you press with a fingertip. Rest again, uncovered, for 10 minutes.

In a large saucepan or deep fat fryer, heat the oil to 375°F (190°C). Holding the square of parchment, transfer each doughnut to the pan, one at a time, being careful not to handle the dough or splash hot oil. Cook in small batches for about 1½ minutes on each side until golden brown. Remove the doughnuts from the oil using a slotted spoon and drain on paper towels, then let cool on a wire rack. Slide a sheet of foil under the rack to catch any drips of glaze later on.

For the dipping glaze, put the lemon juice and confectioners'/icing sugar in a saucepan set over medium heat, stir and simmer for 3–5 minutes until syrupy. Remove from the heat and, one at a time, dip each doughnut in the syrup to coat completely. Remove with a slotted spoon and transfer to the wire rack to set. To prepare the frosting, put the confectioners'/icing sugar in a bowl and add the lemon juice gradually (you may not need it all), along with a few drops of food coloring, stirring until you have a smooth thick frosting. Spoon into a piping bag and pipe drizzles on top of the doughnut, then decorate with sugar sprinkles. Leave to set before serving.

Gluten-free Berry Doughnuts

1⅓ cups gluten-free all-purpose baking flour plus 1½ teaspoons baking powder and ¾ teaspoon xantham gum OR 160 g gluten-free self-raising flour

⅔ cup/140 g ground almonds

1 teaspoon baking powder

scant ½ cup/85 g sugar

½ teaspoon salt

2 eggs, beaten

4 tablespoons/60 g butter, softened

1 cup/250 ml plain yogurt

1 teaspoon vanilla extract

2 tablespoons dried raspberry pieces

2 tablespoons dried strawberry pieces

3 tablespoons dried cranberries

FOR THE BLUEBERRY GLAZE

1 generous cup/120 g fresh blueberries

1⅓ cups/200 g confectioners'/icing sugar, sifted

FOR THE STRAWBERRY GLAZE

1½ cups/180 g hulled and quartered fresh strawberries

1⅓ cups/200 g confectioners'/icing sugar, sifted

3 x 12-hole mini doughnut pans, greased

a piping bag with a large round tip/nozzle (optional)

MAKES 36 MINI DOUGHNUTS

For people who are allergic to gluten or wheat, doughnuts are an often-missed treat. These little baked doughnuts, made with gluten-free flour and almonds, are the perfect solution! Bursting with berries and coated in a strawberry or blueberry glaze, they are sure to be a hit. You can vary the flavor of the recipe easily too—see the variation below for gluten-free lemon treats.

Preheat the oven to 350°F (180°C) Gas 4.

Sift the flour into a large mixing bowl. Add all the remaining doughnut ingredients and beat to a smooth batter with a stand mixer or electric hand whisk. Spoon the mixture into the prepared doughnut pans. This is easiest done by transferring the batter to a piping bag and piping it into each hole. Bake in the preheated oven for 10–15 minutes, until the doughnuts are golden brown. If you don't have three doughnut pans, you can bake them in batches, washing the pan between each batch. Remove from the oven and turn the doughnuts out onto a wire rack to cool. Slide a sheet of foil under the rack to catch any drips of glaze later on.

For the blueberry glaze, gently heat the blueberries with 1 tablespoon of water in a saucepan until the berries burst and release their juices. Pass the blueberries through a strainer/sieve to remove the skins, then return the juice to the pan with the confectioners'/icing sugar and heat until the liquid reduces slightly and becomes syrupy. One by one, coat half of the doughnuts in the blueberry syrup, removing them from the pan with a slotted spoon and returning them to the wire rack. Once set a little, coat them with a second coat of glaze. Prepare the strawberry glaze using the same method and double-coat the remaining doughnuts. Leave them all to set completely before serving.

VARIATION: LEMON DOUGHNUTS For gluten-free lemon doughnuts, simply omit the dried berries and add the grated zest of 1 lemon to the dough. To make the lemon drizzle frosting, mix together the ⅔ cup/100 g confectioners'/icing sugar and enough of the lemon juice to form a smooth thick frosting. Spoon into a piping bag fitted with a small round tip/nozzle and drizzle lines over the doughnuts. If you do not have a piping bag, you can drizzle the frosting over with a spoon.

Raspberry Ring Doughnuts

These dainty doughnuts are bursting with a sharp raspberry flavor. The frosting is made with fresh raspberry juice rather than food coloring, which gives a vibrant color as well as adding extra flavor. I have topped them with fresh raspberries and red edible glitter, but you could decorate simply with sprinkles or dried raspberry pieces, if you prefer.

2⅓ cups/300 g self-rising/
self-raising flour
1 teaspoon baking powder
⅓ cup/70 g sugar
½ teaspoon salt
2 eggs, beaten
3 tablespoons/50 g butter, softened
1 cup/250 ml raspberry yogurt
1 teaspoon almond extract
fresh raspberries, to decorate
red edible glitter, to decorate (optional)

FOR THE FROSTING
1½ cups/100 g fresh raspberries
2 cups/300 g confectioners'/icing
sugar, sifted

*3 x 12-hole mini doughnut
pans, greased*

MAKES 36

Preheat the oven to 350°F (180°C) Gas 4.

Sift the flour into a large mixing bowl. Add all the remaining doughnut ingredients (except the raspberries and glitter) and beat to a smooth batter with a stand mixer or electric hand whisk. Spoon the mixture into the prepared doughnut pans. This is easiest done by transferring the batter to a piping bag and piping it into each hole. Bake in the preheated oven for 10–15 minutes until the doughnuts are golden brown. If you don't have three doughnut pans, you can bake them in batches, washing the pan between each batch. Remove from the oven and turn the doughnuts out onto a wire rack to cool. Slide a sheet of foil under the rack to catch any drips of glaze later on.

For the frosting, put the raspberries in a fine mesh strainer/sieve set over a bowl and use the back of a spoon to push them through the mesh to release their juice. Discard the seeds. Put the confectioners'/icing sugar into a small mixing bowl and add the raspberry juice gradually (you may not need it all), stirring until you have a smooth thick frosting. Spread a layer of frosting over the top of each doughnut using a round-bladed knife and decorate with a whole raspberry. Sprinkle with the glitter, if using, and return to the wire rack to set completely before serving.

Coconut Doughnuts

Coconut rum and fluffy shredded coconut make a tropical topping for these light doughnuts. They are baked in the oven rather than fried, so are not quite so naughty. Decorate in pink and white for a fun twist inspired by retro coconut ice candy!

2⅓ cups/300 g self-rising/
self-raising flour
1 teaspoon baking powder
scant ½ cup/85 g soft light
brown sugar
½ teaspoon salt
2 eggs, beaten
3 tablespoons/50 g butter, softened
1 cup/250 ml milk
1 tablespoon coconut rum

FOR THE COCONUT GLAZE
2⅗ cups/400 g confectioners'/
icing sugar, sifted
½ cup/130 ml coconut milk
1 tablespoon coconut rum

FOR THE TOPPING
½ cup/80 g soft shredded coconut
pink food coloring

*3 x 6-hole doughnut pans, greased
a piping bag with a large
round tip/nozzle*

MAKES 18

Preheat the oven to 350°F (180°C) Gas 4.

Sift the flour into a large mixing bowl. Add all the remaining doughnut ingredients and beat to a smooth batter with a stand mixer or electric hand whisk. Spoon the mixture into the prepared doughnut pans. This is easiest done by transferring the batter to a piping and piping it into each hole. Bake in the preheated oven for 10–15 minutes or until golden brown. If you don't have three doughnut pans, you can bake them in batches, washing the pan between each batch. Remove from the oven and turn the doughnuts out onto a wire rack to cool. Slide a sheet of foil under the rack to catch any drips of glaze later on.

Divide the shredded coconut equally between two bowls. Using a few drops of food coloring, tint half of the coconut pink and leave the remaining half white.

For the coconut glaze, put the confectioners'/icing sugar, coconut milk and rum in a saucepan set over medium heat and simmer for 3–5 minutes until the liquid reduces slightly and becomes syrupy. Remove from the heat and, one at a time, dip each doughnut in the syrup to coat completely. Remove with a slotted spoon and transfer to the wire rack. Sprinkle over the shredded coconut while the glaze is still sticky, coating half of the doughnuts with pink coconut and half with white. Leave to set before serving.

Caramel Ring Doughnuts

These fudge flavored doughnuts are delicious and light as they are baked rather than fried. Topped with a buttery toffee glaze and fudge pieces, they are a caramel-lover's dream. If you only have one doughnut pan, you can bake the doughnuts in batches, washing the pan between each batch.

2⅓ cups/300 g self-rising/
self-raising flour
1 teaspoon baking powder
scant ½ cup/85 g soft light
brown sugar
½ teaspoon salt
2 eggs, beaten
3 tablespoons/50 g butter, softened
½ cup/125 ml milk
½ cup/125 ml plain yogurt
1 teaspoon vanilla extract
3½ oz./80 g fudge, cut into
small pieces, to decorate

FOR THE CARAMEL GLAZE
4 tablespoons/60 g butter
½ cup plus 1 tablespoon/115 g soft
light brown sugar
⅔ cup/160 ml milk
3 cups/440 g confectioners'/icing
sugar, sifted

3 x 6-hole doughnut pans, greased

MAKES 18

Preheat the oven to 350°F (180°C) Gas 4.

Sift the flour into a large mixing bowl. Add all the remaining doughnut ingredients (except the fudge pieces) and beat to a smooth batter with a stand mixer or electric hand whisk. Spoon the mixture into the prepared doughnut pans. This is easiest done by transferring the batter to a piping bag and piping it into each hole. Bake in the preheated oven for 10–15 minutes until the doughnuts are golden brown. If you don't have three doughnut pans, you can bake them in batches, washing the pan between each batch. Remove from the oven and turn the doughnuts out onto a wire rack to cool. Slide a sheet of foil under the rack to catch any drips of glaze later on.

For the caramel glaze, put the butter and sugar in a small saucepan and heat gently until the sugar has dissolved. Remove the pan from the heat, let cool slightly and then add the milk and return to the heat, stirring until well combined. Add the confectioners'/icing sugar and beat over the heat until you have a smooth toffee glaze. Remove the pan from the heat and, one at a time, dip each doughnut in the glaze to coat completely. Remove with a slotted spoon and transfer to a wire rack, then sprinkle over the fudge pieces whilst the glaze is still sticky (it is best to do this in batches as the glaze may set quickly). Leave to set before serving.

Buttermilk Glazed Ring Doughnuts

I love the sour flavor of buttermilk so I have used it in both the doughnut batter and the glaze to give these doughnuts an extra delicious flavor. You can decorate these simple doughnuts with pretty sugar flowers or sugar sprinkles for a delicate effect.

2⅓ cups/300 g self-rising/self-raising flour
1 teaspoon baking powder
scant ½ cup/85 g sugar
½ teaspoon salt
2 eggs, beaten
3 tablespoons/50 g butter, softened
1 cup/250 ml buttermilk
1 teaspoon vanilla extract
sugar flowers, to decorate

FOR THE BUTTERMILK GLAZE
2 cups/300 g confectioners'/icing sugar, sifted
⅓ cup plus 1 tablespoon/90 ml buttermilk
1 teaspoon vanilla bean paste or vanilla extract

3 x 6-hole mini doughnut pans, greased

MAKES 18

Preheat the oven to 350°F (180°C) Gas 4.

Sift the flour into a large mixing bowl. Add all the remaining doughnut ingredients (except the sugar flowers) and beat to a smooth batter with a stand mixer or electric hand whisk. Spoon the mixture into the prepared doughnut pans. This is easiest done by transferring the batter to a piping bag and piping it into each hole. Bake in the preheated oven for 10–15 minutes until the doughnuts are golden brown. If you don't have three doughnut pans, you can bake them in batches, washing the pan between each batch. Remove from the oven and turn the doughnuts out onto a wire rack to cool. Slide a sheet of foil under the rack to catch any drips of glaze later on.

For the buttermilk glaze, put the confectioners'/icing sugar, buttermilk and vanilla in a small mixing bowl and mix together thoroughly, ensuring that there are no lumps. One at a time, dip the top of each doughnut into the glaze and return to the wire rack. Decorate with sugar flowers while the glaze is still sticky and then leave to set before serving.

WACKY WAYS

Doughnut Popcorn

Do not be intimidated by the recipe quantity being 150! These are the teeniest tiniest doughnuts, injected with jelly and coated in sugar, perfect for serving in a popcorn cone.

6½ tablespoons/100 ml milk, warm

1¼ teaspoons/4 g fast-action dried yeast

1½ tablespoons/20 g granulated sugar

1 cup plus 3 tablespoons/150 g all-purpose/plain flour, plus extra for dusting

⅔ cup/80 g white bread/strong flour

½ teaspoon salt

1 egg, beaten

2 tablespoons/30 g butter, softened

1 teaspoon vanilla extract

sunflower oil, for greasing and frying

6 heaped tablespoons seedless raspberry jelly/jam

superfine/caster sugar, for dusting

2 baking sheets

a piping bag with a round tip/nozzle

a small kitchen syringe (needle removed)

a 1¼-inch/3-cm round cookie cutter (optional)

paper popcorn cones, to serve (optional)

MAKES ABOUT 150 (SERVES 6)

Whisk together the warm milk, yeast and sugar in a pitcher/jug and leave in a warm place for about 10 minutes until a thick foam has formed on top of the milk. Meanwhile, sift the flours into a large mixing bowl, add the salt, eggs, butter and vanilla and stir together, then pour in the yeast mixture. Using a stand mixer fitted with a dough hook, mix the dough on a slow speed for 2 minutes, then increase the speed and knead for about 8 minutes until the dough is soft and pliable. Alternatively, knead the dough by hand for 15 minutes. The mixture will be very soft but should not be sticky, so dust with flour if needed.

Cover 2 baking sheets with baking parchment and lightly dust with flour. Take very small pieces of dough, about the size of a bean, and roll into balls. The easiest way to do this is to roll the dough out and cut out 1¼-inch/3-cm circles using a round cutter, then cut each circle into quarters and roll each quarter into a ball. Place the balls on the floured parchment and cover with a clean damp kitchen towel and leave to rest for 10 minutes, and then let rise in a warm place for about 35–45 minutes, covered in lightly-greased plastic wrap, until the dough has doubled in size and holds an indent when you press with a fingertip. Rest again, uncovered, for 10 minutes.

In a large saucepan or deep fat fryer, heat the oil to 375°F (190°C). Holding the sheet of parchment, transfer the doughnuts to the pan, about 30 at a time, being careful not to handle the dough or splash hot oil. Cook for about 45 seconds on each side until golden brown. Remove the doughnuts from the oil using a slotted spoon and drain on paper towels.

Put the sugar on a plate and, when cool enough to handle, roll the doughnuts in it to coat. Spoon the jelly/jam into a piping bag and pipe into the syringe. Inject a small amount of jelly/jam into each doughnut, refilling the syringe using the piping bag, as necessary. Serve in popcorn cones, if using.

Giant Doughnut Birthday Cake

For a doughnut lover, what could be a nicer birthday surprise than receiving a giant doughnut as a birthday cake? You will need a giant doughnut pan to make these cakes, which come in two parts so the halves can be sandwiched together, but you could also use two saverin molds or standard ring cake pans. Add a rich chocolate glaze and a few candles or sparklers and you have the perfect celebration cake.

2½ cups/320 g self-rising/
self-raising flour
scant ½ cup/90 g sugar
¼ teaspoon baking soda/
bicarbonate of soda
2 heaped tablespoons dulce de leche
1 teaspoon vanilla extract
1 cup/250 ml plain yogurt
2 tablespoons/30 ml milk
2 eggs, beaten
3 tablespoons/50 ml corn oil
sugar sprinkles, to decorate

FOR THE CREAM FILLING
1 tablespoon caramel syrup
1 teaspoon vanilla extract
1 cup/250 ml heavy/double cream

FOR THE CHOCOLATE GLAZE
4 tablespoons/60 g butter
3½ oz./100 g plain chocolate,
6 tablespoons/100 ml heavy/
double cream
1 scant cup/115 g confectioners'/
icing sugar, sifted

a 10-inch/25-cm giant doughnut
cake pan, greased

MAKES 1 CAKE

Preheat the oven to 350°F (180°C) Gas 4.

Sift the flour into a large mixing bowl, then add the sugar, baking/bicarbonate of soda, dulce de leche, vanilla, yogurt, milk, eggs and corn oil and beat together with an electric hand whisk. Divide the cake mixture between the 2 pans and bake in the preheated oven for 20–25 minutes until they spring back to your touch and a skewer inserted into the thickest part of the cake comes out clean. Turn the cakes out onto a wire rack to cool.

To make the filling, add the caramel syrup and vanilla to the cream and whip to stiff peaks with an electric hand whisk. When the cakes have cooled level them, if necessary, and then use a round-bladed knife to spread the cream over the top of one of the halves. Invert the other half and place it on top, curved side up, to create a rounded doughnut shape.

For the chocolate glaze, melt the butter, chocolate and cream in a saucepan set over a gentle heat. Remove from the heat and mix in the confectioners'/icing sugar using a wooden spoon, beating hard to remove any lumps. Spread the glaze over the cake and decorate with sugar sprinkles and candles or sparklers. Serve or store in the fridge if not being eaten straight away.

Doughnut Croquembouche

What more decadent way to celebrate a special occasion than with a giant tower of doughnuts! Decorate with sugar flowers for a spectacular centrepiece at any celebration.

1⅔ cups/200 g self-rising/
self-raising flour
⅓ cup/60 g sugar
1 teaspoon baking powder
a pinch of salt
1 large egg plus 1 egg white
⅔ cup/150 ml milk
2 tablespoons plain yogurt
3 tablespoons/50 g butter, melted and
cooled, plus extra for greasing
1 tablespoon rosewater

FOR THE GLAZE
2 cups/300 g confectioners'/icing
sugar, sifted
3–4 tablespoons milk
1 tablespoon plus 1 teaspoon/
20 ml rosewater

TO ASSEMBLE
3 cups/450 g royal icing
mix/sugar, sifted
1 tablespoon rosewater
rice paper flowers

a doughnut maker
a sheet of clean thin card measuring
roughly 24 x 17 inches/60 x 40 cm
scissors and transparent sticky tape
a cake stand or serving plate
a piping bag with a large
star tip/nozzle

MAKES 1 TOWER
(APPROX 45 DOUGHNUTS)

For the doughnuts, sift the flour into a large bowl, then add the sugar, baking powder, salt, whole egg, milk, yogurt, melted butter and rosewater and beat to a smooth batter with an electric hand whisk. In a separate clean bowl, whisk the egg white to stiff peaks, then fold into the batter. Spoon the mixture into a pitcher/jug. Preheat the doughnut maker and grease with butter then pour batter into the holes. Cook in batches for about 3–4 minutes until they are golden brown on both sides, then transfer to a wire rack to cool. The doughnuts will be soft when you remove them from the doughnut maker but will firm up as they cool. Repeat with all of the remaining batter to make approximately 45 doughnuts. Slide a sheet of foil under the rack to catch any drips of glaze later on.

Put the glaze ingredients in a saucepan and heat gently until you have a thin frosting with no lumps. Remove from the heat and, one at a time, dip each doughnut in the syrup to coat completely. Remove with a slotted spoon and transfer to the wire rack to set.

Roll the cardboard into a cone shape and secure with sticky tape, then trim the bottom so it sits flat on a surface. You should be left with a cone which is about 10 inches/25 cm tall and has a base diameter of 6 inches/15 cm.

Put the royal icing mix/sugar and rosewater in a mixing bowl with ⅓ cup/80 ml of water and beat with an electric hand whisk until you have a thick frosting which holds stiff peaks when you lift the beaters out of the mixture. If the frosting is too soft, add a little more sugar and if it is too stiff, add a little extra water. Spoon the frosting into a piping bag and pipe a circle of frosting onto your serving plate or cake stand which has the same circumference as the base of your cone, and then place the cone securely on top. Next, pipe a line of frosting around the cone, roughly 1¼ inches/3 cm up from the base, which will secure the first layer of doughnuts. Arrange a circle of doughnuts around the cone, pressing them into the frosting, so that the sides of each doughnut are almost touching. Pipe another ring of frosting onto the cone about 1¼ inches/3 cm above the top of the first doughnut layer and arrange the next layer of doughnuts. Repeat, creating layers of doughnuts until you have reached the top of the cone. Trim away the top of the cone to just above the height of the doughnuts and place a single doughnut on top. Pipe stars of the remaining frosting around the base and into the gaps between the doughnuts and decorate with rice paper flowers.

Doughnut Pops

These doughnut pops offer the perfect bite-sized doughnut on a skewer—for when three doughnuts are needed rather than one! Flavored with a hint of orange and lemon, you can serve these doughnuts simply rolled in sugar, or why not decorate with melted white chocolate and sugar sprinkles for a pretty party treat.

¾ cup/200 ml milk, warm

¼ oz./7 g fast-action dried yeast

2½ tablespoons/30 g granulated sugar

2⅓ cups/300 g all-purpose/plain flour, plus extra for dusting

1¼ cups/160 g white bread/strong flour

½ teaspoon salt

2 eggs, beaten

4 tablespoons/60 g butter, softened

grated zest of 2 lemons

grated zest of 2 oranges

sunflower oil, for greasing and frying

superfine/caster sugar, for coating

30 squares of baking parchment

q ¾-inch/2-cm round cookie cutter

a piping bag with a round tip/nozzle

wooden skewers

MAKES 26 SKEWERS

Whisk together the warm milk, yeast and sugar in a pitcher/jug and leave in a warm place for about 10 minutes until a thick foam has formed on top of the milk. Meanwhile, sift the flours into a large mixing bowl, add the salt, eggs, butter and zest and stir together, then pour in the yeast mixture. Using a stand mixer fitted with a dough hook, mix the dough on a slow speed for 2 minutes, then increase the speed and knead for about 8 minutes until the dough is soft and pliable. Alternatively, knead the dough by hand for 15 minutes. The mixture will be very soft but should not be sticky, so dust with flour if needed.

Lay the squares of baking parchment on a tray and lightly dust with flour. Roll out the dough to 1¼ inch/3 cm thickness and stamp out about 80 small portions using the cookie cutter. Shape each into a ball and place two or three on each square of baking parchment. Cover with a clean damp kitchen towel and leave to rest for 10 minutes. Reshape the balls and then let rise in a warm place for about 35–45 minutes, covered in lightly-greased plastic wrap, until the dough has doubled in size and holds an indent when you press with a fingertip. Rest again, uncovered, for 10 minutes.

In a large saucepan or deep fat fryer, heat the oil to 375°F (190°C). Holding the square of parchment, transfer the doughnuts to the pan, a few at a time, being careful not to handle the dough or splash hot oil. Cook in small batches for about 1½ minutes on each side until golden brown. Remove the doughnuts from the oil using a slotted spoon and drain on paper towels.

Put the sugar on a plate and, when cool enough to handle, roll each of the doughnut balls in the sugar to coat completely. Thread three doughnuts onto each skewer and serve.

Pistachio Triangle Doughnuts

These doughnuts may look fairly classic from the outside but inside they are bursting with a delicious pistachio cream. They are made using a triangular cutter, but you could use any shaped cutter of your choice. Roll in sugar and pistachio crumb for a pretty effect.

¾ cup/200 ml milk, warm
¼ oz./7 g fast-action dried yeast
2½ tablespoons/30 g granulated sugar
2⅓ cups/300 g all-purpose/plain flour, plus extra for dusting
1¼ cups/160 g white bread/strong flour
½ teaspoon salt
2 eggs, beaten
4 tablespoons/60 g butter, softened
½ cup/60 g shelled and finely chopped pistachios
sunflower oil, for greasing and frying

FOR THE PISTACHIO CREAM
2 tablespoons/30 g butter, softened
½ cup/60 g shelled pistachios
½ cup/60 g confectioners'/icing sugar, sifted
1¼ cups/300 ml heavy/double cream

FOR THE PISTACHIO SUGAR
½ cup/60 g shelled pistachios
¾ cup/150 g superfine/caster sugar

26 small squares of baking parchment
1½-inch/4-cm triangular cookie cutter
a piping bag with a round tip/nozzle

MAKES 26

Whisk together the warm milk, yeast and sugar in a pitcher/jug and leave in a warm place for about 10 minutes until a thick foam has formed on top of the milk. Meanwhile, sift the flours into a large mixing bowl, add the salt, eggs, butter and chopped pistachios and stir together, then pour in the yeast mixture. Using a stand mixer fitted with a dough hook, mix the dough on a slow speed for 2 minutes, then increase the speed and knead for about 8 minutes until the dough is soft and pliable. Alternatively, knead the dough by hand for 15 minutes. The mixture will be very soft but should not be sticky, so dust with flour if needed.

Lay the squares of baking parchment on a tray and lightly dust with flour. Roll out the dough to 1¼ inch/3 cm thickness and cut out 26 triangles, re-modeling the dough scraps if necessary. Place each triangle on a square of baking parchment. Cover the doughnuts with a clean damp kitchen towel and leave to rest for 10 minutes. Reshape the triangles and then let rise in a warm place for about 35–45 minutes, covered in lightly-greased plastic wrap, until the dough has doubled in size and holds an indent when you press with a fingertip. Rest again, uncovered, for 10 minutes.

In a large saucepan or deep fat fryer, heat the oil to 375°F (190°C). Holding the square of parchment, transfer each doughnut to the pan, one at a time, being careful not to handle the dough or splash hot oil. Cook in small batches for about 1½ minutes on each side until golden brown. Remove the doughnuts from the oil using a slotted spoon and drain on paper towels.

To make the pistachio sugar, blitz the pistachios to a fine dust in a food processor. Add the sugar, blend again briefly to combine and then transfer to a shallow dish. While still warm, roll each doughnut in pistachio sugar to coat thoroughly. Use a round teaspoon handle to poke a hole in the doughnut and move it around to make a cavity inside.

For the pistachio cream, blitz the butter, pistachios and confectioners'/icing sugar to a smooth paste in a food processor. Whip the cream until it almost holds stiff peaks then add the pistachio paste and whisk again until the cream is stiff. Spoon the cream into a piping bag and pipe into each doughnut. Serve or store in the fridge if not eating straight away.

Rose Heart Doughnuts

These heavenly heart-shaped doughnuts, topped with rose-scented icing and filled with whipped cream delicately flavored with rose petals, are perfect for Valentine's Day.

¾ cup/200 ml milk, warm
¼ oz./7 g fast-action dried yeast
2½ tablespoons/30 g granulated sugar
1 tablespoon rose syrup or rosewater
2⅓ cups/300 g all-purpose/plain flour, plus extra for dusting
1¼ cups/160 g white bread/strong flour
½ teaspoon salt
2 eggs, beaten
4 tablespoons/60 g butter, softened
sunflower oil, for greasing and frying
crystallized rose petals, to decorate

FOR THE FROSTING
1½ cups/225 g confectioners'/icing sugar, sifted
2 tablespoons rose liqueur
pink food coloring
1–2 tablespoons rosewater

FOR THE ROSE CREAM
a small handful of fresh rose petals
2 tablespoons confectioners'/icing sugar
1 tablespoon rose syrup
1¼ cups/300 ml heavy/double cream, whipped to stiff peaks

12 small squares of baking parchment
a 3-inch/8-cm heart cookie cutter
a piping bag with a round tip/nozzle

MAKES 12

Whisk together the warm milk, yeast, sugar and rosewater in a pitcher/jug and leave in a warm place for about 10 minutes until a thick foam has formed on top. Sift the flours into a mixing bowl, add the salt, eggs and butter and stir together, then pour in the yeast mixture. Using a stand mixer fitted with a dough hook, mix the dough on a slow speed for 2 minutes, then increase the speed and knead for 8 minutes. Alternatively, knead the dough by hand for 15 minutes. The mixture will be soft and pliable but should not be sticky, so dust with flour if needed.

Lay the squares of baking parchment on a tray and lightly dust with flour. Roll out the dough to 1¼ inch/3 cm thickness and cut out 12 hearts, re-modeling the dough scraps if necessary. Place each heart on a square of baking parchment. Cover the hearts with a clean damp kitchen towel and leave to rest for 10 minutes, and then let rise in a warm place for about 35–45 minutes, covered in lightly-greased plastic wrap, until the dough has doubled in size and holds an indent when you press with a fingertip. Rest again, uncovered, for 10 minutes.

In a large saucepan or deep fat fryer, heat the oil to 375°F (190°C). Holding the square of parchment, transfer each doughnut to the pan, one at a time, being careful not to handle the dough or splash hot oil. Cook in small batches for about 1½ minutes on each side until golden brown. Remove the doughnuts from the oil using a slotted spoon and drain on paper towels. When cool enough to handle, use a round teaspoon handle to poke a hole in the doughnut and move it around to make a cavity inside.

For the rose cream, remove and discard the green ends of the petals and then blitz them in a food processor with the confectioners'/icing sugar and rose syrup to form a paste. Fold the paste into the whipped cream, spoon into a piping bag and pipe into the cavity in each doughnut.

For the frosting, put the confectioners'/icing sugar in a bowl with the rose liqueur and a few drops of food coloring and stir to combine. Gradually add the rosewater (you may not need it all), until you have a smooth thick frosting. Spread the frosting on top of the doughnuts in a heart shape and sprinkle over the crystallized rose petals. Serve or store in the fridge if not eating straight away.

Bacon Maple Doughnuts

You are going to have to trust me on this one—I know that the combination of maple syrup and bacon will not appeal to all of you, but for those of you who like bacon and syrup pancakes for breakfast, these doughnuts are for you. The bacon adds a lovely salty kick to counter the sweet maple syrup, making these doughnuts an ideal brunch treat (although I would happily eat them at any time of day!). You can buy ready cooked bacon pieces in the supermarket and they work really well in this recipe.

¾ cup/200 ml milk, warm
¼ oz./7 g fast-action dried yeast
¼ cup/60 ml pure maple syrup
2⅓ cups/300 g all-purpose/plain flour, plus extra for dusting
1¼ cups/160 g white bread/strong flour
½ teaspoon salt
2 eggs, beaten
4 tablespoons/60 g butter, softened
sunflower oil, for greasing and frying
½ cup/50 g real bacon bits/crispy bacon pieces

FOR THE MAPLE FROSTING
2 tablespoons maple syrup
3⅓ cups/500 g confectioners'/icing sugar, sifted

18 small squares of baking parchment
a ¾-inch/2-cm round cookie cutter

MAKES 18

Whisk together the warm milk, yeast and maple syrup in a pitcher/jug and leave in a warm place for about 10 minutes until a thick foam has formed on top of the milk. Meanwhile, sift the flours into a large mixing bowl, add the salt, eggs and butter and stir together, then pour in the yeast mixture. Using a stand mixer fitted with a dough hook, mix the dough on a slow speed for 2 minutes, then increase the speed and knead for about 8 minutes until the dough is soft and pliable. Alternatively, knead the dough by hand for 15 minutes. The mixture will be very soft but should not be sticky, so dust with flour if needed.

Lay the squares of baking parchment on a tray and lightly dust with flour. Divide the dough into 16 portions and, dusting your hands with flour, roll into balls. Using the cookie cutter, cut out a hole from the centre of each dough ball to create a ring. Place each ring on a square of baking parchment. Combine the cut-out dough and mould into balls to make further rings—you should be able to make 18 in total. Cover the doughnuts with a clean damp kitchen towel and leave to rest for 10 minutes, and then let rise in a warm place for about 35–45 minutes, covered in lightly-greased plastic wrap, until the dough has doubled in size and holds an indent when you press with a fingertip. Rest again, uncovered, for 10 minutes.

In a large saucepan or deep fat fryer, heat the oil to 375°F (190°C). Holding the square of parchment, transfer each doughnut to the pan, one at a time, being careful not to handle the dough or splash hot oil. Cook in small batches for about 1½ minutes on each side until golden brown. Remove the doughnuts from the oil using a slotted spoon and drain on paper towels.

Put the maple syrup and confectioners'/icing sugar in a small saucepan with 4 tablespoons water and heat gently, stirring, until you have a smooth thick frosting. Dip the top of the doughnuts into the frosting and then sprinkle with the bacon pieces while the frosting is still sticky. Leave to set before serving.

Bombolini

For lovers of the classic breakfast spread Nutella, the Italians have created the perfect doughnut. The Bombolini is a light dough filled with a chocolate nougatine cream and these are my take on the Italian recipe. Hazelnut butter is available in good health food shops and online. It is a hazelnut version of peanut butter and is truly delicious!

¾ cup/200 ml milk, warm
¼ oz./7 g fast-action dried yeast
2½ tablespoons/30 g granulated sugar
2⅓ cups/300 g all-purpose/plain flour, plus extra for dusting
1⅓ cups/170 g white bread/strong flour
½ teaspoon salt
2 eggs, beaten
4 tablespoons/60 g butter, softened
1 generous tablespoon hazelnut butter
sunflower oil, for greasing and frying
3½ oz./100 g milk chocolate, melted
⅓ cup/50 g toasted hazelnuts, chopped

FOR THE CREAM FILLING
1 generous cup/270 g chocolate hazelnut spread (such as Nutella), at room temperature
¾ cup/200 ml crème fraîche
1 generous tablespoon hazelnut butter

32 small squares of baking parchment

a piping bag with a round tip/nozzle

MAKES 32

Whisk together the warm milk, yeast and sugar in a pitcher/jug and leave in a warm place for about 10 minutes until a thick foam has formed on top of the milk. Meanwhile, sift the flours into a large mixing bowl, add the salt, eggs, butter and hazelnut butter and stir together, then pour in the yeast mixture. Using a stand mixer fitted with a dough hook, mix the dough on a slow speed for 2 minutes, then increase the speed and knead for about 8 minutes until the dough is soft and pliable. Alternatively, knead the dough by hand for 15 minutes. The mixture will be very soft but should not be sticky, so dust with flour if needed.

Lay the squares of baking parchment on a tray and lightly dust with flour. Divide the dough into 32 portions and, dusting your hands with flour, shape each portion into a ball and place on a square of baking parchment. Cover the doughnuts with a clean damp kitchen towel and leave to rest for 10 minutes. Reshape the balls and then let rise in a warm place for about 35–45 minutes, covered in lightly-greased plastic wrap, until the dough has doubled in size and holds an indent when you press with a fingertip. Rest again, uncovered, for 10 minutes.

In a large saucepan or deep fat fryer, heat the oil to 375°F (190°C). Holding the square of parchment, transfer each doughnut to the pan, one at a time, being careful not to handle the dough or splash hot oil. Cook in small batches for about 1½ minutes on each side until golden brown. Remove the doughnuts from the oil using a slotted spoon and drain on paper towels. When cool enough to handle, use a round teaspoon handle to poke a hole in the doughnut and move it around to make a cavity inside.

For the cream filling, beat together the chocolate hazelnut spread, crème fraîche and hazelnut butter until creamy. Spoon the cream into a piping bag and pipe into the cavity in each doughnut. To decorate, drizzle the doughnuts with the melted chocolate and sprinkle over the toasted hazelnuts.

Cruellers

Cruellers are light doughnuts made with either a cake or choux batter and piped into elegant star rings. To ensure that the doughnuts hold their shape you need to chill them in the freezer for a short while before frying. They are particularly popular in Germany where they are sold with a lemon or rum glaze. Sehr lecker (very tasty)!

3⅓ cups/300 g self-rising/self-raising flour, plus extra for dusting
1 teaspoon baking powder
⅓ cup/70 g sugar
¼ teaspoon salt
2 eggs, beaten
3 tablespoons/50 g butter, softened
1 teaspoon vanilla extract
1 cup/250 ml plain yogurt
sunflower oil, for frying

FOR THE GLAZE
freshly squeezed juice of 2–3 lemons
2 cups/250 g confectioners'/icing sugar, sifted

2 baking sheets (small enough to fit in your freezer), lined with baking parchment

a piping bag with a large star tip/nozzle

MAKES 16

Sift the flour into a large mixing bowl. Add all the remaining ingredients (except the frying oil) and beat to a smooth batter with an electric hand whisk. Spoon the mixture into the piping bag. Dust the prepared baking sheet with flour and pipe circles of dough onto the sheet about 3 inches/8 cm in diameter. Put the baking sheet in the freezer to chill for 10 minutes.

Fill a large saucepan or deep fat fryer 4 inches/10 cm deep with oil and heat it to 375°F (190°C). Gently remove the cruellers from the parchment and transfer to the pan, a few at a time, being careful not to splash hot oil. Cook on each side for about 2 minutes until golden brown. Remove one crueller from the oil and cut it open to ensure the cake dough is cooked all the way through. When satisfied they are cooked, remove the doughnuts from the oil using a slotted spoon and drain on paper towels and let cool on a wire rack. Slide a sheet of foil under the rack to catch any drips of glaze later on.

For the dipping glaze, put the lemon juice and confectioners'/icing sugar in a saucepan set over medium heat, stir and simmer for 3–5 minutes until syrupy. For a thin syrup coating use the juice of 3 lemons or for a white frosting use 2. Drizzle the lemon glaze over the cruellers and leave to set before serving.

Churros with Hot Chocolate Sauce

These crispy fried churros are a variety of doughnut popular in Spain and South America. They are made with a cake batter rather than a yeast dough and fry very quickly in hot oil. Due to their quick preparation time, they are often sold in street markets from carts and are always best eaten just after cooking. The traditional way to serve them is with a thick hot chocolate to dip the Churros into. Flavored with hints of mandarin and cinnamon, these delicate doughnuts are sure to disappear as soon as you serve them.

3⅓ cups/300 g self-rising/ self-raising flour
1 teaspoon baking powder
⅓ cup/70 g sugar
¼ teaspoon salt
2 eggs, beaten
grated zest of 2 mandarins
2 teaspoons ground cinnamon
3 tablespoons/50 g butter, softened
1 teaspoon vanilla extract
1 cup/250 ml plain yogurt
sunflower oil, for frying

FOR THE HOT CHOCOLATE
1 cup/250 ml milk
3½ oz./100 g spiced dark chocolate (such as Aztec or Maya Gold)
3½ oz./100 g milk chocolate
1 cinnamon stick
a pinch of ground red chile/ hot chilli powder

FOR THE CINNAMON SUGAR
⅔ cup/120 g sugar
2 teaspoons ground cinnamon

a piping bag with a large star tip/nozzle

MAKES 24

Sift the flour into a large mixing bowl. Add all the remaining ingredients (except the frying oil) and beat to a smooth batter with an electric hand whisk. Spoon the batter into the piping bag.

Fill a large saucepan or deep fat fryer 4 inches/10 cm deep with oil and heat it to 350°F (180°C). Pipe the mixture into the pan in lengths of about 4 inches/10 cm, holding the piping bag in one hand and scissors in the other. Use the scissors to cut the dough at the desired length, being careful not to splash hot oil. Fry the churros in batches of 5, cooking for about 5 minutes and turning frequently until golden brown all over. Remove one churros from the oil and cut it open to ensure the cake dough is cooked all the way through. When satisfied they are cooked, remove the churros from the oil using a slotted spoon and drain on paper towels.

Put the cinnamon and sugar on a plate and mix together. Toss the warm churros in the sugar mixture to coat evenly.

For the hot chocolate sauce, put the milk, chocolate, cinnamon stick and chile/chilli in a saucepan and heat gently until the chocolate has melted. Remove the cinnamon stick, pour into a serving bowl and serve with the churros.

Sopapillas

These little doughnuts are popular the world over in variations of this recipe—I believe their origins lie in Latin America but I have been served very similar honey puffs at Christmas markets in Germany. The classic way to serve them is dusted with confectioners' sugar and drizzled with a little extra honey. Sometimes they are even served in place of bread to accompany savory soups and casseroles. Whatever the true origins of these dainty fried delights, one thing is sure; served warm, they are simply irresistible.

1¾ cups/220 g self-rising/self-raising flour, sifted plus extra for dusting
1 teaspoon baking powder
¼ teaspoon salt
1 teaspoon vanilla extract
1 tablespoon honey, plus extra to serve
3 tablespoons/50 g butter, softened
sunflower or vegetable oil, for frying
confectioners'/icing sugar, for dusting

MAKES ABOUT 60

Put the flour, baking powder, salt, vanilla, honey and butter in a large mixing bowl and blend with an electric hand whisk. Gradually add ½ cup/125 ml water until you have a very soft, but not sticky, dough. Wrap the dough in plastic wrap and chill in the fridge for about 30 minutes.

Dust a clean work surface with flour and roll out the dough to ¼ inch/½ cm thick—it is easiest to do this in batches, rolling out a quarter of the dough at a time. Cut the dough into diamond shapes about 2 inches/5 cm in length.

In a large saucepan or deep fat fryer, heat the oil to 375°F (190°C). Add the sopapillas to the pan in batches, being careful not to splash hot oil, and fry for 3 minutes on one side and then turn over and cook them for a further minute on the other, until golden brown all over. Remove them from the oil using a slotted spoon and drain on paper towels.

While still warm, dust the sopapillas with confectioners'/icing sugar. Serve drizzled with a little runny honey if you wish.

These doughnuts will keep for about 3 days if stored in an airtight container.

Yum Yums

These classic American doughnut twists are made with a yeast dough, which is folded to create air pockets and makes these doughnuts really light.

¾ cup/200 ml milk, warm

¼ oz./7 g fast-action dried yeast

2½ tablespoons/30 g granulated sugar

2⅓ cups/300 g all-purpose/plain flour, plus extra for dusting

1¼ cups/160 g white bread/strong flour

½ teaspoon salt

2 eggs

1 teaspoon vanilla extract

7 tablespoons/110 g butter, softened

sunflower oil, for greasing and frying

FOR THE GLAZE

2 cups/250 g confectioners'/icing sugar, sifted

1 teaspoon vanilla extract

14 small rectangles of baking parchment

MAKES 14

Whisk together the warm milk, yeast and sugar in a pitcher/jug and leave in a warm place for about 10 minutes until a thick foam has formed on top of the milk. Meanwhile, sift the flours into a large mixing bowl, add the salt, eggs, vanilla and 4 tablespoons/60 g of the butter and stir together, then pour in the yeast mixture. Using a stand mixer fitted with a dough hook, mix the dough on a slow speed for 2 minutes, then increase the speed and knead for about 8 minutes until the dough is soft and pliable. Alternatively, knead the dough by hand for 15 minutes. The mixture will be very soft but should not be sticky, so dust with flour if needed.

Leave the dough to rest for 10 minutes, then roll out on a flour-dusted surface to form a rectangle measuring 10 x 14 inches/25 x 35 cm. Spread the remaining butter gently over the dough using your finger tips. With the shortest edge of the rectangle toward you, fold the bottom third up. Turn the dough 180°, and again fold the bottom third up so that it rests on top of the first fold and all the butter is inside the dough. Leave to rest for 10 minutes covered by a clean damp kitchen towel. Roll out the dough again, to the same size, and fold the thirds in the same way. Rest again, covered, for 10 minutes. Roll out the dough for a final time to a 12 x 16-inch/30 x 40-cm rectangle but this time fold the two outside edges into the centre of the dough so that they meet in the middle, then fold the dough in half again so that the middle join is hidden inside the dough. Cut the dough into 14 slices and then, holding each one at the unopened end, twist the two open ends around each other to make the classic yum yum shape. Lay the rectangles of baking parchment on a tray and dust with flour. Place one twist on each piece of parchment and let rise in a warm place for about 35–45 minutes, covered in lightly-greased plastic wrap, until the dough has doubled in size. Rest again, uncovered, for 10 minutes.

In a large saucepan or deep fat fryer, heat the oil to 375°F (190°C). Holding the square of parchment, transfer each doughnut to the pan, one at a time, being careful not to handle the dough or splash hot oil. Cook in small batches for about 1½ minutes on each side until golden brown. Remove the doughnuts from the oil using a slotted spoon and drain on paper towels, then let cool on a wire rack. Slide a sheet of foil under the rack to catch any drips of glaze later on.

Put the glaze ingredients in a saucepan with 3–4 tablespoons water and heat, stirring, until thin and syrupy. Spoon the glaze over the yum yums and let set before serving.

Austrian Apricot Doughnuts

These delicious ìKrapfenî—doughnuts filled with apricot jam and dusted with confectioners' sugar—are traditionally served in Austria at Carnival time. These are my version, with a tangy apricot purée. You can serve any left-over purée alongside the doughnuts for dipping. If you are short of time, substitute with apricot jelly or store-bought apricot purée.

¾ cup/200 ml milk, warm
¼ oz./7 g fast-action dried yeast
2½ tablespoons/30 g granulated sugar
2⅓ cups/300 g all-purpose/plain flour, plus extra for dusting
1¼ cups/160 g white bread/strong flour
½ teaspoon salt
2 eggs, beaten
4 tablespoons/60 g butter, softened
grated zest of 2 lemons
sunflower oil, for greasing and frying
confectioners'/icing sugar, for dusting

FOR THE APRICOT FILLING
8 ripe fresh apricots, pitted and chopped
⅔ cup/130 g granulated sugar
freshly squeezed juice of 1 large lemon
1 teaspoon vanilla extract

16 small squares of baking parchment

a piping bag with a round tip/nozzle

MAKES 16

To make the apricot filling, put the chopped apricots in a saucepan with the sugar, lemon juice and vanilla and simmer until the fruit is soft. Purée in a food processor and set aside to cool.

Whisk together the warm milk, yeast and sugar in a pitcher/jug and leave in a warm place for about 10 minutes until a thick foam has formed on top of the milk. Meanwhile, sift the flours into a large mixing bowl, add the salt, eggs, butter and lemon zest and stir together, then pour in the yeast mixture. Using a stand mixer fitted with a dough hook, mix the dough on a slow speed for 2 minutes, then increase the speed and knead for about 8 minutes until the dough is soft and pliable. Alternatively, knead the dough by hand for 15 minutes. The mixture will be very soft but should not be sticky, so dust with flour if needed.

Lay the squares of baking parchment on a tray and lightly dust with flour. Divide the dough into 16 portions and, dusting your hands with flour, shape each portion into a ball and place on a square of baking parchment. Cover the doughnuts with a clean damp kitchen towel and leave to rest for 10 minutes. Reshape the balls and then let rise in a warm place for about 35–45 minutes, covered in lightly-greased plastic wrap, until the dough has doubled in size and holds an indent when you press with a fingertip. Rest again, uncovered, for 10 minutes.

In a large saucepan or deep fat fryer, heat the oil to 375°F (190°C). Holding the square of parchment, transfer each doughnut to the pan, one at a time, being careful not to handle the dough or splash hot oil. Cook in small batches for about 1½ minutes on each side until golden brown. Remove the doughnuts from the oil using a slotted spoon and drain on paper towels.

When cool enough to handle, use a round teaspoon handle to poke a hole in the doughnut and move it around to make a cavity inside. Spoon the apricot purée into the piping bag and pipe it into the cavity in each doughnut. Dust the doughnuts with confectioners'/icing sugar to serve.

Index